CONFEDERATE AIR FORCE

CONFEDERATE AIR FORCE

PETER R MARCH

Acknowledgements

I would like to record my deep gratitude to Ian MacFarlane, who introduced me to the CAF, and the late Dr Charles Lewis who provided his SNJ-5 for my first air-to-air photography at Harlingen in 1980. Subsequently Fay and Marion Gregory, Steve Sevier and Ken Laird have all generously flown their aircraft for numerous photo sorties. I am indebted to the former CAF Executive Director Ralph Royce and Development Director Herschel Whittington for their unstinting help over the past five years, and the CAF Chief Photographer Bill Crump for his helping hand.

It is impossible to individually name and thank the many CAF colonels who have assisted with the photography, either as pilots of display aircraft, the subjects for air-to-air sorties or for providing me with a steady camera platform. I must, however single out Russ Anderson who worked so hard to make the necessary complex arrangements to get the CAF aircraft in the air as photo subjects in the short amount of time available during the airshow period. Finally, and by no means least, I would like to record my deep appreciation for the time and support given to me by CAF co-founder Lloyd Nolen and for providing the scene setting introduction to this book. To all the colonels of the CAF, thank you.

Published in 1991 by Osprey Publishing Limited
59 Grosvenor Street, London W1X 9DA

British Library Cataloguing in Publication Data

March, Peter R.
    Confederate Air Force.
    1. United States. Military aircraft. Collections
    I. Title
    623.74606075

ISBN 1 85532 172 6

Editor Tony Holmes
Page design Paul Kime
Printed in Hong Kong

Front cover Former 'screen' enemies fly side by side in a colourful formaton of the coast of Texas. The T-6 Texan/Zero replica regularly strays into the gunsights of the FM-2 Wildcat and FG-1D Corsair during the huge set-piece aerial battles which feature prominantly in the Confederate Air Force's Air Power Demonstrations

Back cover The Confederate's operate a priceless collection of classic fighters and bombers, as can be seen from this panoramic shot of the Harlingen ramp. Many aircraft from state branches of the CAF travel miles to participate in the autumn airshow

Title page The Boeing B-29 Superfortress was the World War 2 weapon that proved decisively that strategic bombing could win wars by smashing the enemy's industrial and military capabilities. The concluding blows of the war — the atomic bombs dropped on Hiroshima and Nagasaki in August 1945 — were dealt by this deadly efficient warplane. The CAF's B-29A Superfortress *Fifi*, was rescued from the Californian desert in 1971, where it had been used by the US Navy as a target for testing modern ballistic missiles. Its restoration to flying condition by a CAF team took just nine weeks and on 2 August 1971 it made its first flight for 17 years from Naval Air Station China Lake to Harlingen, Texas, in 6hr 38 mins

Right P-51D N10601 was the first aircraft obtained by the embryo CAF at Mercedes, Texas, in 1957. Built for the USAAF as 44-73843, it subsequently served with the Royal Canadian Air Force as 9271. It moved with the CAF to be based at Harlingen in 1966, where it has since remained as an active participant in the World War 2 Air Power Demonstrations

For a catalogue of all books published by Osprey Aerospace
please write to:

**The Marketing Department,
Octopus Illustrated Books, 1st Floor, Michelin House,
81 Fulham Road, London SW3 6RB**

Contents

Introduction

In the ten years following the end of World War 2 the greatest aerial armada ever assembled was systematically destroyed – turned into scrap – by government decree. There was no organized programme to preserve for the future even one example of each of the historical aircraft types of that era. Unbelievably, the US Navy Air Museum was not established until 1962 and numerous World War 2 aircraft types were missing from the US Air Force Museum collection. More importantly, not one of these historical machines was officially kept flying. And these were aircraft types which had played a decisive role in defeating and preventing the Axis powers from enslaving the free world in the most disastrous and significant war in history.

A small group of local pilots in the lower Rio Grande Valley of Texas decided to do something about this oversight. We had flown a P-40 Warhawk from our grass airstrip at Mercedes in 1951–52, and when a few of our pilot friends saw a P-51 Mustang for sale in 1957, we decided to pool our resources and buy it. A loosely defined organization was formed to share the pleasure and expense of maintaining this fighter. The new outfit was christened when someone painted the title Confederate Air Force on the side of the P-51. The only thing that remained was to commission one and all a 'colonel' in our brand new five-man air force. This embodied the right amount of noble purpose and humorous nonsense.

The Mustang was followed a short time later by an F8F Bearcat, the last of a long line of propellor driven fighters of both the Army Air Force and US Navy.

By 1960 we were being invited to fly our fighters at military bases around the country and it became obvious that these aeroplanes had special meaning for many people and were very popular even in the early years. Therefore, it was decided that, if possible, we would acquire a complete collection of ten famous American fighters. We figured that we could find them at military surplus bases, but when we went to salvage them, we were faced with scenes of destruction and choas. Just 15 years after the end of the war almost all of the 300,000 US warplanes had already been destroyed. Faced by this, our decision to rebel against the official indifference to the loss of our aviation heritage became more important and more urgent.

In 1960 a P-38 Lightning and an FG-1D Corsair joined the fighter fleet at Mercedes, now renamed Rebel Field. The CAF was chartered as a non-profit making organization in 1961 and it immediately began to grow. By 1963 we had completed the collection of ten fighters when some character came along with a B-25 Mitchell, and we found ourselves in the bomber business as well! The decision was made to expand our goal to include all American World War 2 combat aircraft types, bombers and fighters alike. By 1968 the CAF had outgrown its original grass strip and moved to the former Harlingen Air Force Base ten miles to the east. The 'Ghost Squadron', as it had become known, now had 380 members, 21 aircraft and a large home base on which it could develop further. Four years later the entire collection of US combat aircraft had been completed and the enthusiasm of over 500 dedicated people had produced an almost complete collection of transports and trainers, as well as a unique assortment of former RAF, Luftwaffe, and Japanese aircraft.

By 1974 the CAF airshows had developed into the World War 2 Air Power Demonstration, depicting the major air combat actions of the conflict. A decade later the CAF had spread its wings worldwide and had accumulated a fleet of over 140 aircraft, representing 62 different types flown during World War 2. Just as importantly, the organization had over 7000 colonels in 82 CAF Wings, Squadrons, and Detachments across North America, Australia, New Zealand, and Europe.

Now, in 1991, the CAF is beginning a new and challenging phase in its development. We have begun a new partnership with the citizens of Midland and Odessa in west Texas that will see the CAF grow and prosper into the world's leading centre for the preservation of World War 2 aviation history and heritage. At Midland-Odessa International Airport we are building a world-class museum that will function as learning centre for historic military aviation, a library and research centre and the world's foremost restoration and maintenance facility for World War 2-vintage aircraft. It will also be the new headquarters for the CAF, operated by the largest and most professional 'civilian flying team' in the world.

This magnificent collection of photographs by Peter R March will certainly give you a taste of our World War 2 Air Power Demonstration, and I hope that it will promote an interest in the Confederate Air Force and encourage you to visit us at our new home at Midland-Odessa International Airport.

Lloyd P Nolen
Co-founder and former Chief of Staff
Confederate Air Force
January 1991

Sadly, Lloyd Nolan passed away in April 1990. This volume on the Confederate Air Force is dedicated to him.

Fighter Muscle

Designed by North American Aviation for the RAF, the NA73, powered by a 1150 hp Allison V-1710 engine, was built in just 117 days as the prototype Mustang, making its first flight on 26 October 1940 at Mines Field, Los Angeles. It was soon to be ordered for the USAAF, and when re-engined with the Rolls-Royce/Packard Merlin, the Mustang was dubbed 'the best all-round American-built fighter of World War 2'

Above & right Fitted with long-range fuel tanks, the P-51 had a greater cruising range than any other USAAF fighter and was therefore brought into use as an escort fighter for the strategic bomber force of B-17s and B-24s, accompanying the heavies on their high altitude daylight raids over Europe. *Gunfighter II*, shown here being flown by General Regis Urschler, is a P-51D, serial 44-73264/N5428V, maintained by the CAF

Left A line-up of P-51Ds at Harlingen in October 1981 when it was common for 12 to 15 Mustangs to take part in the annual airshow

Above The CAF's first P-51 and *Gunfighter II* in a mixed fighter formation with a P-39 Airacobra, P-47 Thunderbolt and a third Mustang, appearing at the 1988 Wings over Houston Airshow organized by the CAF

Right The Republic P-47 Thunderbolt was designed in 1940 as a long-range escort fighter. It entered service in 1943 operating with the 8th Air Force in Europe, and nicknamed the *Jug*, it was the largest and heaviest single-engined fighter of the war. It flew 546,000 sorties and it is claimed that it destroyed 7067 enemy aircraft in Europe and the Pacific. Over 16,000 P-47s were built for the USAAF together with the RAF, Free French and the Soviet Air Force. The CAF Thunderbolt (45-53436) is a P-47N, and it was obtained from the Nicaraguan AF and delivered to Mercedes on 7 February 1963. It was rebuilt after crashing at Vero Beach, Florida, on 29 April 1971

Below Produced in 1939 by the Bell Aircraft Corporation, the P-39 Airacobra single-seat fighter was revolutionary in design as the 1200 hp Allison V-1710-E engine was located behind the pilot, driving the propellor by an extension shaft beneath the cockpit to a gearbox in the nose. A 37 mm cannon fired through the hollow airscrew shaft and additional machine guns were mounted in the fuselage and wings. It was one of the smallest fighters of World War 2 and the first to feature a tricycle undercarriage. Of the 10,000 P-39s produced from 1939 to 1944 nearly half were sent via lend-lease to the Soviet Air Force where they were mainly employed against German tanks. The CAF's P-39Q is painted in Russian markings and operated by the Central Texas Wing at San Marcos. In service as 42-19597 it was abandoned by the USAF in New Mexico after an accident at Hobbs AFB, and after restoration by Don Hull at Sugarland, Texas, between 1969 and 1972, it joined the CAF at Harlingen on 3 December 1974

Above The Bell P-63 Kingcobra was developed in 1941 from a modified P-39 Airacobra fuselage, with redesigned laminar-flow wing, angular tail surface and a more powerful Allison V-1710-93 engine. The basic armament comprised one 37 mm cannon and two 0.50 in guns in the nose and one 0.50 in gun in each wing

Right Bell produced 1725 P-63s but only a few reached USAAF units, the majority going to Russia on lend-lease as tank-busters. Three-hundred were also supplied to the Free French AF. The Kingcobra had a maximum speed of 408 mph and a service ceiling of 43,000 ft

The CAF's P-63F 41171/N6763 photographed over South Padre Island, Texas, in October 1987, was operated as a race aircraft from 1946 until 1978. It was acquired by the Confederate Air Force in 1981 and delivered to Harlingen on 10 August that year

One of the oldest surviving Kingcobras, N191H is seen here being dismantled at Harlingen in October 1990 to facilitate its restoration at another location. A static exhibit at Dallas/Love Field until 1960, P-63A 42-68941 was restored by Col Don Hull at Sugarland to flying condition in 1965. It was amongst the first group of CAF fighters based at Mercedes

Left The P-40 was the last of the famous Curtiss Hawks and it was flown on almost all battle fronts in World War 2. The aircraft was supplied to 28 allied air arms including those of Britain, France, China and Russia, and various models were known as the Tomahawk, Kittyhawk and Warhawk. Apart from the P-51 and P-47, it was produced in greater quantity (13,783) than any other US fighter

Above In December 1941 the P-40 was the standard US Army Air Corps fighter, and a small number managed to get airborne during the Japanese attack on Pearl Harbor. The fighter earned its fame through the actions of General Clâire Chennault's American Volunteer Group (AVG) in China. Known as the *Flying Tigers* (hence the insignia carried on the aircraft), the three squadrons of volunteer pilots helped defend Chinese airfields against the invading Japanese, shooting down over 200 enemy planes in the process. AVG losses amounted to only eight aeroplanes in return

Left In 1941 a Rolls-Royce Merlin 28 was installed in a P-40D Warhawk airframe, replacing the Allison V-1710 to produce the F-model. P-40s of later variants served mainly with USAAF units in the Middle East and Pacific area, but the greater proportion were supplied under lend-lease to Allied nations, notably Britain, Russia, China, South Africa and Australia. Some 2500 Warhawks (mostly P-40Ns) were on USAAF strength in April 1944

Above The CAF's P-40N Warhawk (N1226N), seen here suffering from an over-rich mixture at Airsho '90, was one of the original fighter aircraft obtained by Lloyd Nolen and colleagues at Mercedes in 1965. It was built in 1942 and supplied to the Royal Canadian Air Force (serialled 867) the following year. Acquired by a private owner at Seattle in August 1947, it passed through several hands until 1958 when it moved to Norderland, Texas

Left Although Supermarine Spitfire Mk IX MK297 was purchased by the Confederate Air Force in 1965, it did not find its way to Texas until after the shooting of the *Battle of Britain* film. Built as an LF Mk IXc for the RAF, the Spitfire was supplied to the Royal Netherlands Air Force in June 1947, subsequently moving on to the Belgian Air Force in 1952. After demobilization it was operated in Belgium before crossing the Channel to Film Aviation Services at Elstree (as G-ASSD) on 28 April 1964

Above Since early 1969 MK297 has been active with the CAF fleet, representing the RAF in the Battle of Britain scenario in the Air Power Demonstration. Although it sometimes wears other markings for film work, the Spitfire Mk IX, here photographed in 1980, usually displays the code D-B and markings of an aircraft flown by the late Sir Douglas Bader. MK297 is currently based with Howard Pardue at Breckenridge in Texas

Above Visiting Airsho '90 at Harlingen was Spitfire T.Mk 9 TE308/N308WK. Flown by owner Bill Greenwood from Aspen, Colorado, TE308/N308WK substituted for the CAF's damaged MK297 in the aerial clash with a 'Ju 52', 'He111' and 'Messerschmitt Bf 109'. This trainer was operated by the Irish Army Air Corps from July 1951 until sold to Samuelson Films at Elstree to take part in the *Battle of Britain* film. It was sold to a private owner in Ontario, Canada, in July 1970 and after several further changes reached Bill Greenwood in 1983

Right CAF founder member Col Marvin L 'Lefty' Gardner's P-38L Lightning N25Y is probably one of the USA's best known warbirds. Built in 1944 as a P-38L-5-LO (serial number 44-53254), it was obtained in 1947 by J D Reed at Houston for air racing. He removed the turbo-superchargers, bulky chin radiators and fitted close cowls to resemble the earlier P-38H. It moved to various owners in the 1950s before finally ending up with Vernon Thorpe at Yukon, Oklahoma, in 1963. The following year he agreed to sell the 'Fork-tailed Devil', as the P-38 was known, to Cols Lefty Gardner and Lloyd Nolen for a mere $4000. Painted in a distinctive overall white scheme with red trim, N25Y has since been displayed by Lefty at airshows across the USA for nearly 30 years

Left and overleaf Development of
the unusual North American P-82
Twin Mustang began late in 1943
when there was an urgent need for
very long-range fighters to fly
bomber escort over the Pacific. On
the premise that two P-51 Mustangs
'should be twice as good as one', the
manufacturer used two lengthened
P-51H fuselages and modified port
and starboard wing halves, joined by
a new centre wing and tailplane. The
Twin Mustang was powered by two
1860 hp Allison V-1650 engines.
This configuration provided
a twin-engined aircraft with
a cockpit each for the pilot (left) and
radar operator (right), and a large fuel
capacity, giving a maximum range of
2400 miles. A total of 273 P-82s
were built for the USAF

Above The CAF's P-82B (46-5162) was discovered by CAF Col Ira Haskins at Lackland AFB, Texas, in early 1966. Mounted on a plinth and exposed to the elements for the previous 15 years, the big twin was donated to the CAF in May 1966 and it was taken by road to Kelly AFB, San Antonio, where it was restored for the ferry flight to Harlingen. This flight took place on 31 January 1969 in the hands of Col Joe Algranti. Much of the following decade was spent rebuilding the Twin Mustang and it appeared at CAF airshows again in the 1980s. After a number of flights that were plagued by engine problems, the P-82 stalled and made a crash landing at Harlingen's airshow on 10 October 1987. The damage was soon repaired but the rare fighter has not been able to fly again as it lacks the contra-rotating propellors uniquely fitted to this type

Middle weight Twins

Right Design work on the new aircraft began in 1938 as a private venture by North American, the Mitchell subsequently proving to be one of the war's outstanding bombers. Easily identified with its shoulder gull wing, deep fuselage, twin fins and rudders, tricycle undercarriage and large radial engines, it was for its day heavily armoured with nose, dorsal and ventral gun positions and provision for three more fixed forward-firing guns in the wings

Overleaf Some 11,000 North American B-25 Mitchells were built between 1940 and 1945, of which the USAAF received 9816. They served on every major front during the war with the USAAF, the USN and air forces of the Allies

Right The Confederate Air Force currently has six B-25s on strength, including *Yellow Rose* operated by the Yellow Rose Squadron from San Antonio, Texas. Built as a B-25J (43-27868), it was subsequently converted to a TB-25N trainer. Registered N25YR, it was delivered to the CAF in September 1979 and progressively re-configured as a B-25J

Below Named after Brigadier General Billy Mitchell who was a pioneer advocate of military air power, the B-25 gained notoriety early on its career when the USAAF launched a daring attack on Tokyo. Sixteen B-25s, flown by volunteer crews under the leadership of Lt Col Jimmy Doolittle, took off from the USS *Hornet* as the carrier cruised in the Pacific on 18 April 1942 to bomb the Japanese capital over 700 miles away. This raid had far-reaching psychological effects on both the Americans and the Japanese. President Roosevelt telling the world that Doolittle's raiders had come from a secret base called 'Shangri-La'

The Missouri Wing's B-25 *Show Me* was restored over a three-year period from February 1982, the immaculate bomber, which has an original Norden bomb-sight in the nose, now operating out of Smartt Field/Saint Charles County Airport. A firm favourite with the airshow crowds in Texas, *Show Me* regularly takes part in CAF performances throughout the year

Above Originally designed by Douglas in 1938 as an attack bomber, the A-20 Havoc proved to be a jack-of-all-trades with the USAAF, RAF, Free French and the Soviet Air Force. Over 7300 A-20s were built. The CAF's 322210/T (obtained on 12 September 1966 from Boise, Idaho) was restored in the colour scheme worn by Havocs of south western Pacific units and the markings of the 312th Bomb Group based in New Guinea. Unfortunately, this last airworthy example of the A-20 was lost on 8 October 1988 when the pilot had a fatal heart attack during the airshow at Harlingen

Right The Army Air Corps was so pleased with the drawing board version of the Martin 179 medium bomber that it ordered 1000 without the benefit of a prototype. Although it was named after one of the largest predatory sea birds, the B-26 Marauder initially acquired a bad reputation amongst crews despite having the lowest combat loss ratio of any aircraft in World War 2

Above The B-26 was clearly ahead of its time being high-powered, heavily armed, and possessing a high wing loading that dictated fast landing speeds and long take-off runs. The Marauder incorporated a lot of new technology including a fresh and somewhat untried engine, and an electrically actuated propellor for the first time

Above right The only Marauder still in flyable condition is the CAF's B-26C-20 *Carolyn,* this aircraft being ordered on 28 June 1941 as part of a batch of 175 airframes. Accepted by the Army Air Corps on 24 May 1943, 41-35071 was struck off the USAAF books on 23 April 1945, the aircraft spending its final months in service as a TB-26C trainer. Subsequently converted to civilian use, it was sold for VIP service with Tennessee Gas at Houston. Registered N5546N, it flew as an executive transport from 1953 to 1965, before being purchased by the CAF in November 1967. Left in storage until 1975, the aircraft was eventually restored to airworthy condition in 1984

Below right How did it acquire the name 'Carolyn'? Quite simply a sponsor offered $50,000 for the name of his wife to be printed on the nose, and naturally this offer could not be refused by the CAF!

Right Perhaps the most impressive USAAF 'twin' of World War 2, the Douglas A-26 Invader was also the last of its genre to enter service with the Air Force. Designed by Ed Heinemann prior to Pearl Harbor as a successor to the A-20 Havoc, the prototype A-26 first flew on 10 July 1942 and production Invaders reached the 9th Air Force in Europe in November 1944. With powerful 2000 hp Pratt & Whitney R-2800-27 engines, the A-26 achieved a maximum speed of 355 mph at 15,000 ft, thus making it one of the fastest bombers used by the USAAF in World War 2. Internal storage was provided for a 4000 lb bomb load

Below Typical of the colourful nose art carried by the CAF's bombers, *Daisy Mae* adorns the Razorback Wing's A-26C 44-35643, based today at Pine Bluff, Arkansas. After post-war service with the USAAF, this Invader was operated by the French Air Force for a short time. Converted for corporate transport use in 1963, it was based at Wichita (as N6841D) and in Mannitoba (as C-GCES) from 1973 to 1979. The CAF finally took delivery in October 1979 and it commenced flying in 1984 after restoration at Pine Bluff

Left Sunset at Harlingen with B-25 *Show Me* silhouetted behind the Canadian Warbird Heritage's A-26 C-GHLK/434313, visiting Airsho '90 from Hamilton, Ontario

Above The Hudson is one of the rare examples of a successful military type developed from an existing commerical design – the Lockheed 14 transport. The military version (first flown on 10 December 1938) was built in response to the RAF's requirement for a coastal reconnaissance bomber, over 1500 Hudsons being delivered to Coastal Command and the Royal Australian Air Force during the first years of the war. In 1941 the US Army Air Force, and subsequently the Navy, employed the Hudson on anti-submarine duties. Photographed on recovery to Harlingen in 1980, the CAF Hudson wears an early-war Coastal Command finish

Left Built by Lockheed in January 1945, the PV-2 Harpoon *Fat Cat* was discovered at Marianna Airport, Florida, by colonels of the Cajun Wing. It was ferried to Lafayette, Louisiana, in March 1985 and by October of that year was taking part in airshows at Houston and Harlingen. Sadly this long-range medium torpedo bomber was burnt out in September 1990 following a ground engine fire

Below The B-23 Dragon was developed by Douglas to meet a 1938 Army requirement for a fast medium bomber as a replacement for the B-18 series. Using DC-3 wings and two 1600 hp Wright R-2600-2 engines, it first flew in July 1939, but it did not measure up to the B-25 and B-26, being slower and less adequately armed. Only 38 were built and many served in a variety of utility roles as the UC-67. Following the end of World War 2 many aircraft found their way into airline and corporate fleets, the CAF's B-23 (N62G) being operated as a company transport by Standard Oil and General Electric before being acquired by the Confederates in October 1973

Above When the CAF's Dragon was given a thorough check in the mid 1980s it was found to have major corrosion problems. A full rebuild was decreed and it is progressively being restored to 'as new' condition by the B-23 squadron. It had reached this stage at Harlingen by October 1990

Right Ordered by the US Navy in 1933, the Consolidated Model 28 Catalina featured a parasol-mounted wing without external bracing, together with unique retractable stabilizing floats which folded upwards to become wing-ups in flight. When America entered the war in December 1941, the Catalina was the principal long-range patrol flying boat in service with the US Navy. With over 3290 airframes eventually being built, the PBY served with numerous air arms and with civilian operators in many countries for more than 30 years. The CAF's Catalina (N68756) was built as a PBY-5A in 1944 and served with the US Navy until 1950. Restored in its wartime colours, the Catalina is now assigned to the CAF's Pacific Wing. It was built in 1944 and operated with the US Navy until 1950

Above The Curtiss C-46 Commando was the largest twin-engined cargo transport produced during World War 2. It featured a new type of loading ramp and wide doors that opened upwards making possible the swift loading of motorised equipment under its own power. The C-46's enduring fame was earned flying essential supplies from India to the beleaguered forces in China and Burma over the Himalayan 'Hump', the world's highest mountain ranges. Post-war, many C-46s served as airliners and cargo transports, particularly in South America. The CAF's C-46 (N78774) *Tinker Belle* is operated by the Oklahoma Wing from Oklahoma City

Above right Produced as a commercial airliner, the Douglas DC-3 was operated by the USAAF in large numbers as a wartime troop transport and cargo aircraft. Officially designated C-47 Skytrain by the US Army and known as the Dakota in RAF service, it was affectionately nicknamed the *Gooney Bird*

Below right This C-47, operated by the CAF's Dallas/Fort Worth Wing, proudly wears the markings of a USAAF aircraft that took part in *Operation Overlord*, the D-Day Invasion of France that took place on 6 June 1944

Above The R4D was the US Navy's version of the Douglas DC-3. The CAF obtained this example in 1980 as a standard DC-3, but during restoration the original Navy data plates were discovered. Consequently the aircraft was fully restored as an R4D bearing the Naval Bureau of Aeronautics number (BuNo) 50783. The records showed that it was built in October 1944 and had been used as an anti-submarine warfare (ASW) aircraft, primarily for the training of crews in the use of new equipment. It was one of a group of 35 which were converted on the production line to the US Navy's R4D-6 specification, the '6S' specification denoting that it had been modified for anti-submarine warfare

Right Restored to static display condition at Harlingen, this Douglas C-54D Skymaster (N4470M) was made airworthy shortly before the 1990 Autumn airshow. The first C-54 was flown on 26 March 1942 from Santa Monica, and 952 were subsequently built for the Air Force and a further 211 for the US Navy. This C-54D, built in 1944, was operated by the Pacific Division of Air Transport Command

Naval Wings

The unmistakable gull wing of the Vought F4U Corsair. This fleet fighter first saw action with the US Marines at Guadalcanal on 14 February 1943. It was the first fighter fitted with a 2000 hp engine and using that power became the first US Navy machine to exceed 400 mph in level flight. The Corsair joined Marine and land-based Navy squadrons in October 1942

Left The Corsair fought in every major Pacific battle from 1943 onwards. Over 65,000 sorties were flown and F4Us destroyed 2140 Japanese aircraft for the loss of only 189 in aerial combat – a ratio of 11:1. This FG-1D Corsair (N9964Z) was obtained by the Mercedes, Texas, based CAF in 1960. It crashed at Olathe, Kansas, in 1974 but in 1980 was rebuilt by the LTV Corporation, the restored 'bent-wing' fighter being handed back to the CAF by the Chief Executive of LTV, Paul Thayer, on 14 March 1981

Below Here flying in company with two FM2 Wildcats (an aircraft that it partly replaced in frontline service during World War 2), the F4U also served with distinction in the Korean War. A most unusual Corsair wartime kill was achieved by Lt R R Klingman over Okinawa when his machine chewed off the elevator and rudder of a Japanese aircraft with its propellor after he discovered that his F4U's guns were jammed

Grumman's first torpedo aircraft was a fat-bellied machine powered by the dependable Wright R-2600 engine. The TBF Avenger had a fully enclosed torpedo bay and a dorsal turret at the rear end of the long cockpit glasshouse, but rather than being revolutionary in concept the design placed its merits in simple construction and great strength, with good performance. The first prototype flew on 1 August 1941 and production deliveries commenced in January 1942

Avengers were in action on all fronts during the war. In the Atlantic the Avenger, along with another Grumman aircraft, the Wildcat, went to war against the U-boat menace carrying an array of rockets, bombs and depth charges. Many types of the Avenger featured two .50 calibre wing guns. Special anti-submarine detection radar in the TBM-3E made this variant of particular value to the US Navy in the early post-war years and it became the principal operational version of the Avenger after 1945

Avenger production continued until 1945 by which time a total of 7546 aircraft
had been delivered, over 5000 of these airframes being built by General Motors
as TBMs. Post-war, many surplus examples found their way to conversion as
fire bombers and crop sprayers, whilst the US Navy even used a seven-seat
transport version developed for carrier on-board delivery (COD)

Left The CAF's Curtiss Helldiver, an SB2C-5, saw active service with the US Navy. Originally declared surplus at Corpus Christi, Texas, it was used as a trade-school training aid in Montana until acquired in the early 1960s by Ed Maloney for his Planes of Fame Museum at Ontario, California. It languished there until 1970 when CAF Colonels Nolen, Gardner and Griffin put in a successful bid to buy it for $25,000. It took over 12 months of hard work to restore the SB2C to flying condition and in late November 1971 it was flown from California to Harlingen. For the next ten years it was extensively displayed – until September 1982 when the engine failed on take-off, the resulting stall and crash during the emergency landing resulting in extensive damage

Above Colonels of the West Texas Wing were determined to see the 'Big-Tailed Beast' back in the air so under the leadership of Nelson Ezell, the SB2C's costly restoration was put in hand at Breckenridge, Texas. Finally completed on 27 September 1988, the Helldiver was flown again and appeared a few days later at the Wings over Houston Airshow, now painted in the colours of the USS *Franklin* Air Group

Above Although the first Dauntless was flown in July 1935, deliveries of the definitive SBD-1 version were not made by Douglas until late 1940. Over 5000 aircraft were built before production of the carrier-based scout, dive and torpedo bomber ceased in July 1944. The SBD Dauntless was credited with sinking a greater tonnage of Japanese shipping than any other Allied aircraft of the war

Left One of only a handful of survivors, the CAF's Dauntless was built at the El Segundo factory as an A-24B (42-54532), equivalent to the SBD-5. Post-war it was sold to Mexico as XB-QUC and used for aerial photography until mid 1964. Acquired by Ed Maloney in 1965, it was purchased, like the Helldiver, by the CAF colonels in 1970 and flown to San Antonio, Texas, before subsequently moving on to Harlingen where it has since remained. It was temporarily grounded in 1990 for a major overhaul

Above One of the outstanding naval fighters of World War 2, the Wildcat was Grumman's first monoplane. Powered by a 1050 hp Pratt & Whitney R-1830-66 Twin Wasp, it had a maximum speed of 290 mph. A mid-wing, all-metal aircraft with an armament of two .50-in guns in the fuselage, it had provision for two more in the wings, or two 100 lb bombs beneath the wings. First flown on 2 September 1937, deliveries to the US Navy commenced early in 1940, and it was the standard US Navy fighter at the time of Pearl Harbor, remaining so until the F6F Hellcat and F4U Corsair joined the fleet in 1943

Above right The advent of the small escort carrier led to development of the FM-2 version of the Wildcat, of which 41-F-4 flown by the CAF is an example. It combines the more powerful 1350 hp Wright R-1820-56 Cyclone engine with a lighter airframe to obtain improved take-off performance from the shorter carrier decks. The FM-2 has a taller fin to counteract the increased engine power and the final production batch also had a water-injection system. Wildcats were standard equipment with the majority of the 114 escort carriers in service by 1945

Below right This FM-2 Wildcat (N5833) was acquired by the CAF's San Diego Air Group One from the Yankee Air Corps at Ohio, California, in September 1986. The aircraft was taken by road to Ramona where its rebuild was completed by Chuck Hall, who piloted the FM-2 on its first flight for 35 years on 24 April 1987. The Wildcat has since made regular airshow appearances

The Bearcat was the US Navy's last propellor-driven fighter, the first frontline squadron receiving their factory-fresh aircraft on 21 May 1945. Although it did not see combat whilst in US service, it saw plenty of action in Indo-China with the French *Armée de l'Air* and the Royal Thai Air Force during the 1950s. Powered by the Pratt & Whitney R-2800 engine, the Bearcat had an outstanding performance, especially in the climb (4800 ft per min). It was first flown on 21 August 1944 and achieved a top speed of 424 mph. This F8F-2 (N7825C) was acquired by the CAF on 8 February 1972 and is operated from its headquarters after being rebuilt in the late 1980s at Chino, California

Designed by Grumman, the twin-engined F7F Tigercat was intended for operation from the US Navy's larger 45,000 ton carriers, and although classified as a fighter it operated mainly in the ground-support role. The big single-seat aircraft is powered by two 2100 hp Pratt & Whitney R-2800-22W engines giving a top speed of 424 mph. This example (N7195C) was operated as a firebomber before being restored at Oakland, California, in the early 1980s. It is a regular visitor to CAF airshows from the Kalamazoo Aviation History Museum

Left Hawker Sea Furies like this two-seat T.Mk 20 are frequently flown at CAF organized events. The Sea Fury was the Fleet Air Arm's last piston-engined frontline fighter and saw service with six squadrons in Korea. This T.Mk 20 was used as a target tug in Germany after service as an RN trainer

Above One of a large batch of Sea Fury FB.Mk 11s acquired by Ed Jurist and David Tallichet from the Iraqi Air Force in 1978, N195F was painted to represent an aircraft flown by the Royal Canadian Navy. Sadly it was destroyed in a fatal take-off accident at Harlingen soon after this photograph was taken on 9 October 1981

Tora, Tora, Tora

Left and overleaf The outstanding Mitsubishi A6M Zero-Sen originated from a Japanese Navy specification in 1937 which called for a carrier-borne fighter to succeed the standard A5M. The prototype A6M made its first flight on 1 April 1939 but tests showed it needed a more powerful engine. The aircraft was put into production in 1940 as the A6M2 with the 950 hp Nakajima Sakae 12 air-cooled radial engine. It was known to the JNAF as the *Rei Sentoki*, or Zero-Sen, although the Allies referred to it as the *Zeke*. This new fighter was first used operationally in China, and at Pearl Harbor on 7 December 1941 its speed, range and manoeuvrability took the US forces by surprise. During the first half of 1942 the Zeros of the Striking Force and the Eleventh Air Fleet were more than a match for any of the fighters the Allies could use against them, but they failed at the Battle of Midway Island in June 1942 to save the Japanese carrier force from a calamitous defeat. From 1943 the A6M lost its ascendancy, though the A6M3, with a 1130 hp Sakae 21 engine, remained a formidable weapon and was produced in larger numbers than any other Japanese aircraft. Some 10,000 Zeros were produced by Mitsubishi and Nakajima but few of them survive today and only two are in airworthy condition. This CAF A6M2 Zero, photographed in October 1990, was found in the jungle of Ballale Island in the Solomon Islands by a Canadian some 35 years after it had crashed. It was purchased by the CAF and restored to flying condition, making its first public appearance at the 40th anniversary of VJ Day on 14 August 1985

Left and overleaf When Twentieth Century Fox Studios made the film *Tora, Tora, Tora* in the late 1960s they needed a large number of aircraft for the surprise attack by machines from the Japanese carriers on the US Naval Base at Pearl Harbor on 7 December 1941. The acquisition of 30 airworthy Japanese aircraft was impossible, so replicas had to be used by converting existing types of aircraft. Many of these very realistic replicas have remained together as the *Tora, Tora, Tora* Group to re-enact the Japanese air attack which brought America into World War 2. Twelve North American AT-6s were converted to Zero configuration for the movie, the modifications being completed by Cal-Volair in California. The trainers' long canopy was removed and a new single piece hood fitted. Wheel covers were provided and the rudder shape was modified. An engine intake scoop was installed under the cowl and cut outs were made at the exhaust outlet. A larger spinner was also provided together with a three-bladed propellor. Some of the *Zekes* were further modified with retractable tailwheels and lengthened main undercarriage legs. The replicas were finished in a representative paint scheme of the 1941 period. Just as in the epic film, the *Zeke* replicas' airshow routine includes the extensive use of pyrotechnics and on board smoke systems

Of the replica conversions the Nakajima B5N2 *Kate* dive bomber proved to be the most ambitious project as it made use of both North American AT-6/SNJ and Consolidated Vultee BT-13 airframes. The AT-6 structure was extended by 16-in forward of the firewall to give a less tapered appearance, and the canopy structure was removed and the rear fuselage empennage section was discarded. A new seven-foot fuselage lattice was bolted between the modified AT-6 forward section and the complete rear section of a BT-13. This provided a look-a-like *Kate* fuselage with a completely new canopy made in five sections. The manufacture of nine *Kate* replicas was contracted to Cal-Volair at Long Beach, California. Five of these replicas remain active with members of the *Tora, Tora, Tora* Group today

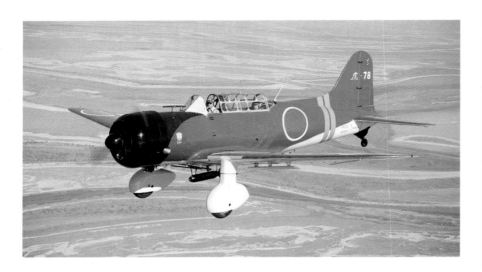

The *Val* replica was based on the Vultee BT-13 Valiant trainer, the basic modification centring around the fitment of a big 550 hp Pratt & Whitney R1340 engine in place of the 450 hp R985, and the lengthening of the rear fuselage just behind the cockpit by two feet. The forward fuselage was re-skinned to match the larger diameter engine, the cockpit edges were raised to reduce the canopy glazed area and the rear canopy was given a swivelled opening to allow the rear gun to move. Extensive use of fibreglass was made to produce the new dorsal fin, rounded wingtips, dive-brakes and wheel spats. Some of the *Vals* were also equipped with swinging bomb arms that actually worked. Nine *Val* conversions were undertaken by Stewart Davis at Long Beach, four of which continue to take part in *Tora, Tora, Tora* displays

Heavy Metal

Right The B-17 Flying Fortress was designed in 1934, first flown on 28 July 1935 and delivered to the USAAC from late 1939. Possessing an impressive range, the Boeing bomber allowed the US to operate strategic bombing missions across all continents. Able to operate in daylight at an altitude in excess of 30,000 ft, it was the mainstay of the Eighth Air Force in England and North Africa

Below B-17 44-83514 *Sentimental Journey*, seen here flying with the PV-2 is sponsored and operated by the CAF Arizona Wing. It joins other heavies in dramatizing the strategic bombing of Europe during the CAF Air Power Demonstrations

Left *Sentimental Journey* was accepted by the Army Air Corps on 27 March 1945, having been built by Douglas, under contract to Boeing, in 1944. It is believed that this aircraft took part in the Berlin Airlift. In 1959, registered N93232, it was converted for use as a fire bomber. Acquired by the CAF in 1978 it has since been progressively restored to its wartime configuration

Above B-17 483872 *Texas Raiders* has been part of the CAF fleet since 1967 and currently flies in the colours of the 381st Bomb Group, 8th Air Force, and is operated by the West Texas Wing. The Flying Fortress was so named from the belief that the heavy armament and defensive guns would give it total protection in the air. Unfortunately this assumption proved to be wrong, and from early in the air war over Europe P-38, P-47 and P-51 long range fighters were required to escort the vast bomber fleet on bombing raids to ward off Luftwaffe fighters

Right In the *Tora, Tora, Tora* sequence of the Air Power Demonstration a lone B-17 (*Texas Raiders*) is attacked by Zeros as it attempts to land at Pearl Harbor. Number three engine trails smoke and the damaged bomber limps away on that fateful day in December 1941

Below The nose art of *Sentimental Journey* depicts the film star Betty Grable in a pin-up pose, which fits the period appearance. The name *'Sentimental Journey'* stems from a state-wide newspaper contest which prompted over 800 entries

Left The concept of a very long range, high altitude and large capacity bomber appeared on Boeing's drawing boards as early as 1937. By 1940 the design was complete and the first flight of the XB-29 took place on 21 September 1942. A total of 3960 B-29s were delivered

Above Named *Fifi*, the CAF B-29 (44-62070) has a starring role in the CAF's Air Power Demonstrations, and it is seen leading a P-40 Warhawk, P-47 Thunderbolt and P-51 Mustang over the CAF Headquarters' Airsho at Harlingen in October 1980

Capable of a range of 3700 miles with a 20,000 lb bomb load, the B-29 was operated solely in the Pacific theatre. From airfields in India and China the B-29 initially flew raids against Japanese targets in south west Asia, but later in World War 2 operated from bases built on the captured islands of Saipan, Guam and the Marianas. From these islands the B-29s staged high-altitude raids on the Japanese homeland itself

On 6 August 1945 and again on 9 August, one bomb dropped by a single B-29 on Hiroshima and another on Nagasaki settled a key issue – there would be no land invasion of Japan. Japan surrendered unconditionally on 15 August 1945

Above An abortive attack on the majestic Super Fortress by a Zero replica is one of the concluding scenarios in the Air Power Demonstration, as the B-29 makes its symbolic raid on Tokyo

Right Keeping the B-29 airworthy is a huge task for the CAF colonels. A team of airframe and powerplant mechanics spend over 300 man-hours checking the bomber's 50 miles of tubing and cables, 144 spark plugs, over 100 functions per engine and 350 for the hydraulics, electrical and control systems, as well as the landing gear. This annual check also involves changing 90 gallons of oil in each engine and five gallons of hydraulic fluid to enable *Fifi* to receive FAA approval for another year's flying

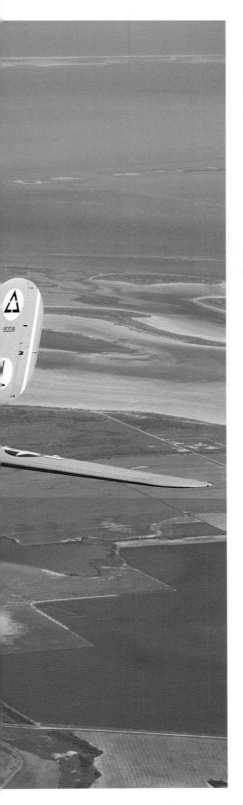

Left The CAF flies the oldest surviving B-24 Liberator, N12905 *Diamond Lil* being only the 24th aircraft to leave Consolidated's production line. It was built for the RAF as an LB-30A patrol bomber, serialled AM927, but when bound for England it suffered an accident. Returned to the manufacturers, it was rebuilt as a corporate personnel transport, spending the rest of the war and some years afterwards in that configuration. It was sold to the Continental Can Company at Morristown, New Jersey, in November 1948 and to Pemex in Mexico in April 1959 as XC-CAY. Acquired by the CAF in 1967, it was flown to Harlingen in May 1968 where it has been based ever since

Above The Consolidated Model 32 B-24 Liberator was manufactured in larger numbers (18,432) and probably flew a wider range of missions than any other US aircraft in World War 2. It was designed in late 1938 as a high-speed, long range bomber and featured the Davis high-aspect ratio wing of constant taper. The prototype XB-24 was first flown at San Diego on 29 December 1939. It had what was then considered a very high wing loading and required skill and expertise for take-offs and landings. The B-24's long range made it especially effective as a strategic bomber across the Pacific

Spanish Luftwaffe

Left, below and overleaf Photographed in October 1987, this Spanish built Messerschmitt Bf 109 – in fact a Hispano Aviacion HA-1112-M1L *Buchon* – was one of four aircraft acquired by the CAF in 1967 and taken to Harlingen after their use in the epic *Battle of Britain* film. Powered by Rolls-Royce Merlin engines in place of the Bf 109's Daimler-Benz DB605, they were operated by the Spanish Air Force until 1965. This aircraft (N8575) was operated by No 471 Squadron at Tablada as C4K-144 and after purchase by the CAF was loaned to Hamish Mahaddie for the *Battle of Britain* film. It was registered to Spitfire Productions Ltd as G-AWHP on 14 May 1968, and to Wilson C Edwards at Big Spring, Texas, as N8575 on 20 February 1969. Fully restored by the CAF with an overhauled engine and modern electronics, it was in action at airshows until 1987. Sadly it crashed on take-off from Harlingen on 19 December 1987 and was burnt out, killing the pilot

Right Another of the quartet of *Buchons* that the CAF colonels purchased from the Spanish Air Force, this aircraft (N109ME) has been stored at Harlingen for many years, and is painted in a Luftwaffe North African desert colour scheme

Like the Me 109, the CAF's Heinkel He 111 is a Spanish built derivative – the CASA-2111E – powered by Rolls-Royce Merlin engines (in place of Junkers Jumos). The He 111 was designed as a transport aircraft in 1933, being derived from the earlier He 70. First flown in 1935, the new bomber was extensively trialed in the Spanish Civil War, 30 He 111s going to Spain in February 1937. In CAF Air Power Demonstrations, the Heinkel He 111 takes part in the opening scene entitled: 'The Spanish Civil War – The first test of Hitler's Luftwaffe'

Serialled T8.B–124 and flying as a trainer with the Spanish Air Force until the late 1960s, this CASA/He 111 was stored at Cuatro Vientos near Madrid until purchased by Doug Arnold's Warbirds of Great Britain and flown to Blackbushe on 21 May 1976 (as G-BDYA). Stored here for 16 months, it was prepared for the long trans-Atlantic flight to its new owners at the CAF, finally departing for Texas on 24 September 1977. Now registered N72615, it was overhauled and quickly joined the CAF's flying display participants operating from the Harlingen headquarters. There is only one other airworthy He 111 survivor

Above The tri-motor Junkers Ju 52 made its debut as a Lufthansa airliner in 1932 and ranks alongside the DC-3 as the world's most famous transport aircraft. It served for over 40 years throughout the world and was the Luftwaffe's mainstay in the transport role during the war. The angular corrugated-skinned transport served on every major front and was affectionately known by Luftwaffe personnel as the *Tante Ju* (Auntie Junkers). Over 4850 of all variants were produced and many continued to serve long after the end of World War 2

Right The CAF's aircraft (N352JU) is one of a hundred Ju 52/3ms built by CASA for the Spanish AF. It is painted in wartime Luftwaffe markings and takes part in the 'Nazi Blitzkrieg on Poland' scenario in the Air Power Demonstration, as does a 'Mercedes staff car' which transports a Field Marshal Goering look-a-like. *Tante Ju* is based at Gary, Indiana, with the South Lake Michigan Wing of the CAF

Designed in 1935 as a high-wing monoplane for German army co-operation, liaison and casualty-evacuation duties, the Fieseler Fi 156 carried a crew of three. The Storch's high-lift devices gave it a remarkably short take-off and landing capability, and with a take-off speed of 32 mph, it could operate from tiny fields. The Fieseler aircraft began to reach Luftwaffe units in the winter of 1937 and was used in every front by the Luftwaffe and carried out invaluable work in all its designed roles. A total of 2549 Fi 156s was produced during the war and production continued post-war by Morane-Saulnier in France as the MS 500 and 502 Criquet, as well as in Czechoslovakia as the K-65 Cap

Developed in 1932, the Focke-Wulf FW44 Stieglitz was built as a primary training and aerobatic aircraft for the fledgling Luftwaffe. It has a Siemens Sh14a seven-cylinder, air-cooled radial engine developing 150 hp, giving it a maximum speed of 115 mph. The type was also built under licence in Sweden. The CAF's Stieglitz, photographed near Harlingen in October 1990, is lovingly cared for by the Rio Grande Valley Wing

Training
for War

North American Aviation Inc entered
the training aircraft field in 1935 with
a privately financed prototype.
Evaluated at Wright Field, the Yale
was regarded as the closest approach
to a tactical aircraft yet achieved in a
trainer. It had a 450 hp Wright
Whirlwind R-985-25 radial engine
and had a fixed undercarriage.
This NA-64 (NX13397) photographed
with the trainer line-up at
Harlingen in 1980, was the first of a
production batch destined for the French
Air Force

Above and right Flown by more military pilots worldwide than any other aircraft, the North American AT-6/SNJ Texan had an unusually long service life. Produced as an advanced trainer in 1938, it was used at USAAF pilot training schools until September 1956. The Texan was used to train nearly 100,000 USAAF and USN pilots during the war and was operated by 34 air arms worldwide. These colourful examples, photographed during CAF Airsho '89, are both former US Navy SNJ-5 advanced trainers.

Above and right This ex-US Navy SNJ-5B retains its former Navy training school markings, while the T-6 Texan flown by Col Steve Gustafson wears rather extravagant Luftwaffe markings. Both were photographed during the spectacular flypast by more than 30 Texans over Harlingen in October 1980. Of particular interest are the long lines of warbirds on the CAF apron waiting their turn in the Air Power Demonstration. Behind them are retired USAF aircraft, including a B-47 Stratojet and C-124 Globemaster, which have long since been removed

Although US Army policy tended to favour the biplane for primary pilot training programmes, the Fairchild PT-19 trainer was built in numbers that approached the prolific Boeing Stearman biplane, and was widely used in US training schools. The PT-19 Cornell had tandem seating in open cockpits, but for use on the Commonwealth Air Training Scheme in Canada a version of the PT-19A was built with a canopy over the two cockpits with blind flying instrumentation. Redesignated PT-26, this example of the Cornell (N261A) is operated from San Antonio, Texas, by the Alamo Wing; behind it is a Consolidated BT-13/SNV Valiant, operated as a basic trainer from 1940 to 1943

Above and right The Boeing Stearman Navy N2S-3 primary trainer and Army Air Corps PT-17 Kaydet were used for primary flight training prior to and during World War 2. Equipped with a 200 hp Continental R-670-5 radial engine, it had a maximum speed of 135 mph and cruising speed of 96 mph. An alternative version, designated PT-18, had a Jacobs R-755-7 radial engine. Production was completed in February 1945 after 10,346 models, in their various configurations, were built. The combination of blue fuselage and yellow wings on the PT-17 was the typical paint scheme for Army primary and basic trainers. This PT-17 (N65666) is flown by the Rio Grande Valley Wing at Harlingen

Above This Beech 18R/AT-11 Kansan (N145SC) has been fully restored by its owner to its original configuration as a 'frustrated' bomber for the Chinese Air Force, and was photographed flying near to Harlingen in October 1989. The AT-11 was developed from the AT-7 in 1941 for bombing and gunnery training. The special navigation equipment was removed and a bomb-bay provided in the fuselage in its place. The nose was remodelled with a bomb-aimer's position along with nose and dorsal guns. Over 1580 Kansans were manufactured

Above right Of the three types of commercial lightplane selected by the Army in 1941 for evaluation in the role of artillery spotting and front line liaison, the Piper Cub was eventually produced in the greatest numbers. Some 3500 L-4 Grasshoppers were built, the L-4s performing their first combat mission when they flew off an aircraft carrier during *Operation Torch*, the invasion of North Africa in 1943

Below right The Stinson AT-19 Reliant was built under lend-lease arrangements for use by the British Fleet Air Arm as an observer/radio trainer and observation aircraft. Photographed in 1989, FK887 was painstakingly restored by pilot/owner Steve Sevier, while FK810 in the background is operated by the CAF's Carolinas Wing from Huntersville, South Carolina. Both Reliants saw wartime service with the Royal Navy in England

Ground Party

The drama of the CAF's Air Power Demonstration includes a ground sequence by 'Nazi soldiers' and 'Luftwaffe Staff Officers' parading before the arrival of Field Marshal Goering in his Ju 52 to survey their devastation in Poland